Deafness

Angela Royston

www.heinemann.co.uk/library

Visit our website to find out more information about **Heinemann Library** books.

To order:

 Phone 44 (0) 1865 888066

 Send a fax to 44 (0) 1865 314091

 Visit the Heinemann Bookshop at www.heinemann.co.uk/library to browse our catalogue and order online.

First published in Great Britain by Heinemann Library, Halley Court, Jordan Hill, Oxford OX2 8EJ, part of Harcourt Education.
Heinemann is a registered trademark of Harcourt Education Ltd.

© Harcourt Education Ltd 2005
The moral right of the proprietor has been asserted.

Editorial: Sarah Shannon and Richard Woodham
Design: Ron Kamen, Victoria Bevan and Celia Jones
Picture Research: Maria Joannou and Kay Altwegg
Production: Amanda Meaden

Originated by Dot Gradations Ltd
Printed and bound in China by South China Printing Company

ISBN 0 431 11222 3
09 08 07 06 05
10 9 8 7 6 5 4 3 2 1

British Library Cataloguing in Publication Data
Royston, Angela
  Deafness – (What's it like?)
  362.4'2

A full catalogue record for this book is available from the British Library.

Acknowledgements
The publishers would like to thank the following for permission to reproduce photographs:
Alamy pp.**10**, **12**; Corbis pp.**6** (Jose Luis Pelaez, Inc.), **17** (Ed Bock), **19** (James W. Porter), **22**, **27** (Duomo); Getty Images pp.**11** (Photodisc), **13** (Photodisc), **14** (Photodisc), **26** (Photodisc); Rex Features p.**23** (Alix/Phanie); Science Photo Library pp.**7** (David Gifford), **8** (BSIP VEM), **15** (BSIP VEM), **16** (Lea Paterson); Tudor Photography pp.**4**, **5**, **9**, **18**, **20**, **21**, **24**, **24**, **25**, **25**, **25**, **25**, **28**, **29**.

Cover photograph of a group of children reproduced with permission of Powerstock/Superstock.

Every effort has been made to contact copyright holders of any material reproduced in this book. Any omissions will be rectified in subsequent printings if notice is given to the publishers.

The publishers would like to thank Fran Simmons for her assistance in the preparation of this book.

The paper used to print this book comes from sustainable resources.

Contents

Words appearing in the text in bold, **like this**, are explained in the Glossary.

 Find out more about what it's like to be deaf at www.heinemannexplore.co.uk

What is deafness?

Most people can hear many kinds of sounds, even very quiet sounds. A person is hard of hearing if they can hear loud sounds only.

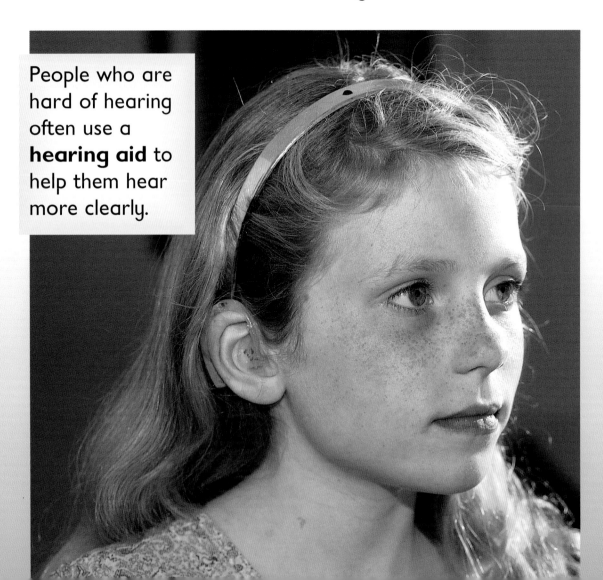

People who are hard of hearing often use a **hearing aid** to help them hear more clearly.

Deaf people use senses other than hearing to find out what is going on.

On TV screen: 08

BOTH: And we are The Cheeky Girls. And this is our Cheeky Dog.

SONY

A person is deaf if they cannot hear well enough to understand what someone is saying. Only a very few deaf people hear nothing at all.

How do you hear?

You hear through your ears. Sounds go into your ear and hit your **eardrum**. The eardrum then passes these sounds further along your ear.

Sounds have to go inside your ear before you can hear them.

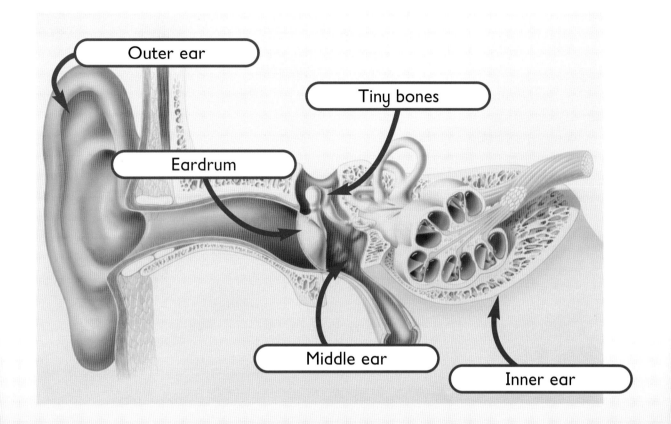

Outer ear

Tiny bones

Eardrum

Middle ear

Inner ear

After reaching the eardrum, sounds pass along tiny bones to the inside of your ear. Here special **nerves** change the sounds into **signals**. You hear a sound when these signals reach your **brain**.

7

What stops you hearing?

You cannot hear properly unless sounds are able to pass through the ear. Wax or **mucus** may sometimes block the ear.

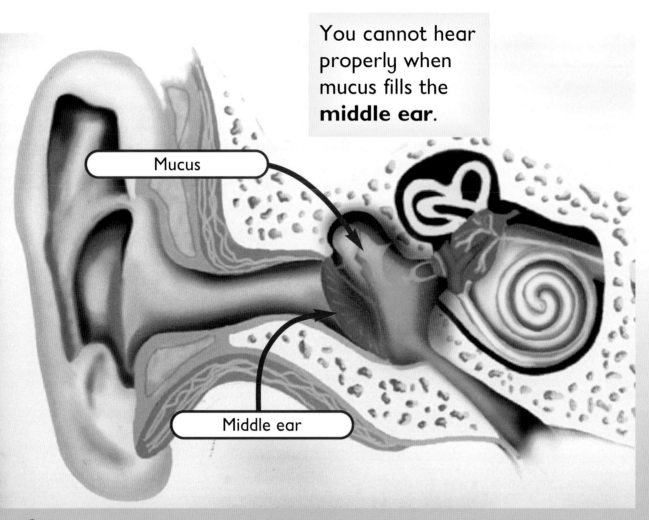

You cannot hear properly when mucus fills the **middle ear**.

Mucus

Middle ear

Some deaf people cannot hear even loud noises.

Nerve deafness is when the **nerves** in the **inner ear** do not work properly. They do not send enough **signals** to the **brain**.

Why are people deaf?

Some people are born deaf. Deafness can be passed on from parents to their children. A mother catching **rubella** whilst **pregnant** can also cause the child to be born deaf.

Ear infections can cause **mucus** to block the **middle ear**. Illnesses such as **measles** and **meningitis** can sometimes damage parts of the ear and cause deafness.

Some illnesses can cause deafness.

Loud noises

A loud noise, such as an aeroplane engine, can damage a person's ears and make them hard of hearing. Some noises, such as explosions, are loud enough to cause deafness.

This drill is loud enough to damage a person's ears.

This man is wearing ear protectors so his ears are not damaged by the noise of the saw.

Many older people are hard of hearing or deaf because their ears have been damaged over time by loud noises.

Helping hearing problems

Some people who are deaf have
a **hearing aid** to help them hear.
The hearing aid picks up sounds
and makes them louder.

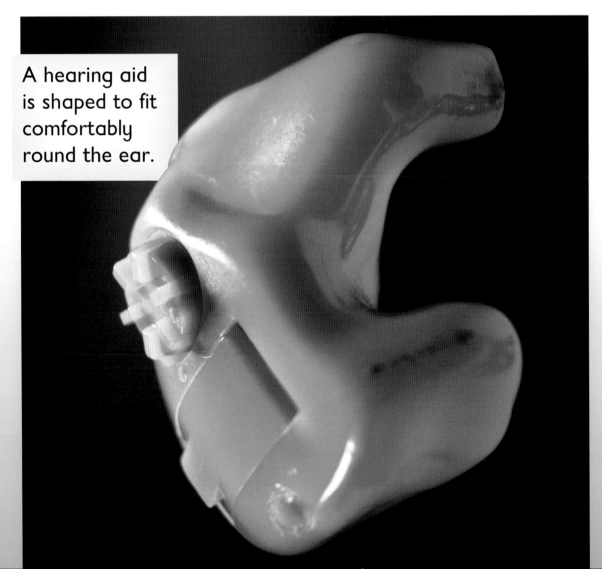

A hearing aid
is shaped to fit
comfortably
round the ear.

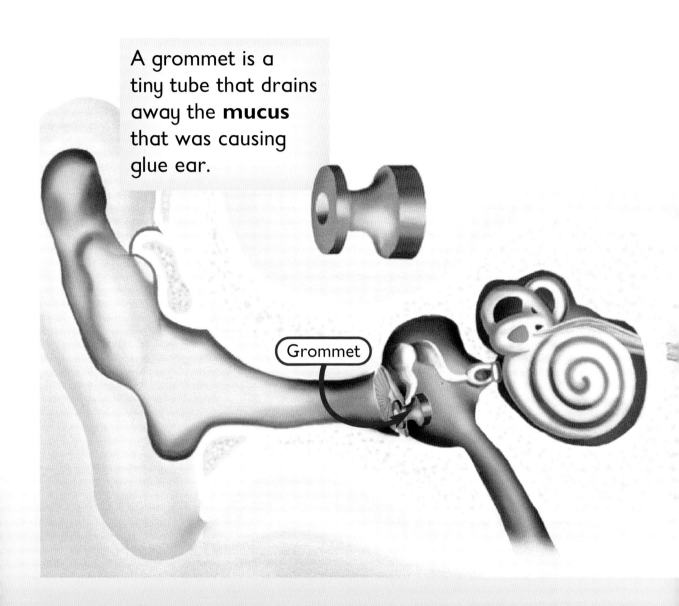

A grommet is a tiny tube that drains away the **mucus** that was causing glue ear.

Grommet

Sometimes a child with **glue ear** may have a **grommet** put into their ear. An **operation** can sometimes help people with **nerve deafness**.

People who are hard of hearing can hear loud sounds but not quiet sounds. They may find it hard to hear somebody talking in a noisy place, such as a crowded **restaurant**.

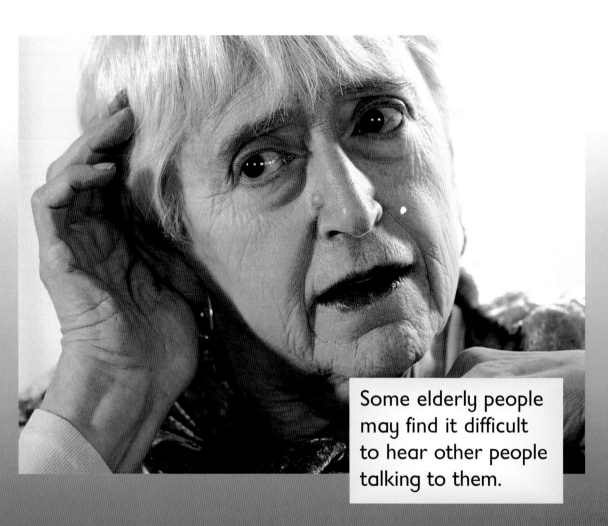

Some elderly people may find it difficult to hear other people talking to them.

When you talk to someone who is hard of hearing, make sure that they can see you. Remember to talk clearly and not too quickly.

Living with deafness

People who are deaf can enjoy many of the same things as everyone else. When they listen to music or watch television, they use special headphones that make the sound louder.

A text telephone shows the words the caller is saying on a screen.

Everyday objects can be changed slightly to help people who do not hear well. For example, lights can be made to flash when the doorbell rings.

Lip reading

Some deaf people learn to understand what you say although they cannot hear the words. They watch the different shapes your lips make as you say different words.

Many deaf people watch how the
expression on your face changes as
you speak. Watching a person's face
can help a deaf person understand
what is being said.

Signing

Some deaf people use their hands and fingers instead of speaking. There are several different **sign languages**. Some hearing people learn to use sign language.

Sign language allows you to speak to someone without making a noise.

Some sign languages use one sign to stand for a whole word. Sign alphabets are also used around the world. A sign alphabet uses a different sign to spell out each letter of a word.

Using sign language

These pictures show the **sign language** for saying the word 'hello'.

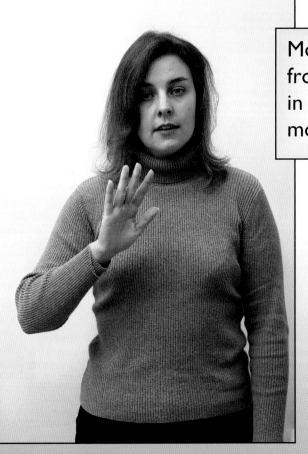

Move your hand from left to right in one clear movement.

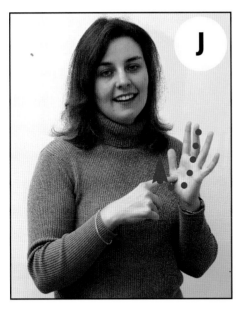

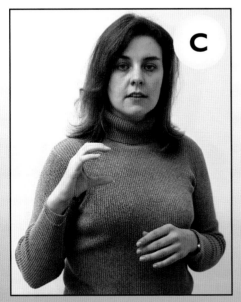

These pictures show how you would use
the sign alphabet to say the name 'Jack'.

25

Sports and games

Deaf children enjoy themselves just as other children do. You do not need to hear for many sports and games, such as running, swimming, board games, and computer games.

Hand signals can be used instead of whistles.

Deaf people can play football and most other team games. They cannot hear the **referee's** whistle, but they can read the hand **signals** the referee makes.

Enjoying life

Many deaf children learn how to play a musical instrument. They enjoy making music by feeling how the instrument **vibrates** when it is played.

A **hearing aid** can also help when playing an instrument.

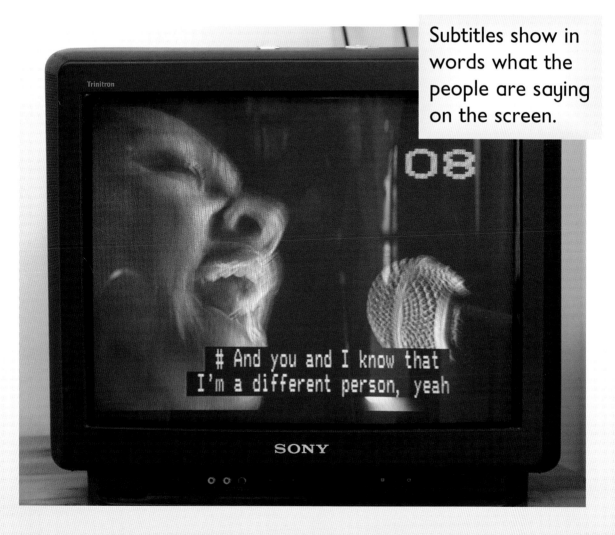

And you and I know that
I'm a different person, yeah

Many objects help people who are deaf. For example, some alarm clocks vibrate when they ring. **Subtitles** help deaf people to follow what is said on films and television programmes.

Find out more

National Deaf Children's Society

Learn about how you or your school can get involved in raising money to help people who are deaf or hard of hearing.

www.ndcs.org.uk

British Deaf Sports Council

This is where to look first if you want to know more about sports for the deaf and hard of hearing.

www.britishdeafsportscouncil.org.uk

Sign Alphabet Translator

Type a word in and an American sign alphabet equivalent is displayed.

www.apples4theteacher.com/translate.html

 Find out more about what it's like to be deaf at www.heinemannexplore.co.uk

Disclaimer

All the internet addresses (URLs) given in this book were valid at the time of going to press. However, due to the dynamic nature of the Internet, some addresses may have changed, or sites may have ceased to exist since publication. While the author and publishers regret any inconvenience this may cause readers, no responsibility for any such changes can be accepted by either the author or the publishers.

Glossary

brain part of the body that controls the rest of your body and with which you think

eardrum part of the ear that vibrates when sounds enter your ear

ear infection illness that fills your middle ear with mucus and gives you earache. Usually the mucus clears when the infection goes.

expression look on your face that shows how you feel

glue ear deafness caused when mucus becomes stuck in the middle ear

grommet small tube used to let mucus drain out of the middle ear

hearing aid object that fits in the ear of someone who is hard of hearing and makes sounds louder so they can be heard

inner ear deepest part of your ear; the nerves that react to sounds are in the inner ear

measles illness that can damage the nerves in your inner ear

meningitis illness that makes a thin covering over your brain become swollen; this swelling can cause deafness

middle ear part of your ear between your eardrum and the inner ear

mucus sticky liquid made by the body

nerve part of the body that carries messages to and from the brain

nerve deafness not being able to hear because nerves in the ear no longer work

operation treatment involving opening up part of a person's body in order to repair something that is wrong

pregnant carrying an unborn baby

referee person who makes sure that a game is played fairly

restaurant place where you can buy and eat a meal

rubella illness that gives you a fever and a rash

sign language way of talking to someone using your hands and fingers

signal message or sign

subtitles words on a television or cinema screen that show what the people are saying on the screen

vibrate shake very quickly

More books to read

Woodhouse, Jayne, *Lives and Times: Helen Keller* (Heinemann Library, 1998)

Spilsbury, Louise, *What Does It Mean To Be Deaf?* (Heinemann Library, 2002)

Index

Titles in the What's It Like? series include:

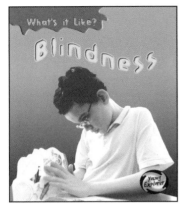

Hardback   0 431 11223 1

Hardback   0 431 11225 8

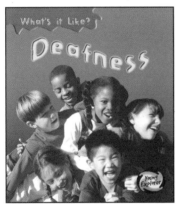

Hardback   0 431 11222 3

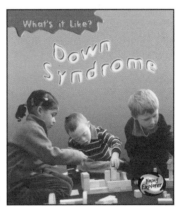

Hardback   0 431 11226 6

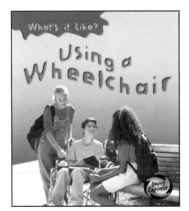

Hardback   0 431 11224 X

Find out about the other titles in this series on our website www.heinemann.co.uk/library